STOP MANAGING YOUR SALES PROCESS LIKE YOUR SEX LIFE

STOP MANAGING YOUR SALES PROCESS LIKE YOUR SEX LIFE

By:

Erika L. Lunceford

STOP MANAGING YOUR SALES PROCESS LIKE YOUR SEX LIFE

STOP MANAGING YOUR SALES PROCESS LIKE YOUR SEX LIFE

I'm Erika Lunceford and I've been an active participant in the corporate arena for over 20 years and I've worked in Sales for over 10 of those years. What I've walked away with are valuable lessons learned from costly mistakes I've made or I've witnessed. I've also had the formidable opportunity to be a key contributor of the sales team that did a lot of things right and held the client's names and logos in their personal portfolio to prove it.

We're all adults here. As I've walked through my personal journey in the world of entrepreneurship over the past five years, I have had the opportunity to see the typical sales process from a different perspective. Although, overall the goal is the same; gain new business, retain clients and upsell existing clients, I've realized that we are sometimes guilty of having a sales strategy that is very similar to how someone would

STOP MANAGING YOUR SALES PROCESS LIKE YOUR SEX LIFE

manage their sex life. I don't want my previous statement to be misconstrued as a bad thing because I'm the first to admit that a sex life is perhaps one of the most fulfilling aspects of being an adult. I will also admit that sometimes the way we manage our sex life is not ideal for our personal growth and fulfillment and definitely using similar strategies to run our business can be...let's just say, less than smart. I'll show you what I mean as we venture through this book together.

While, what I share may be simple, hopefully, you'll identify with one of the sales types or better yet, maybe you won't. The objective is to call attention to the areas that can use improvement, especially for those who are new to the idea of sales. At the end of the day, we're all sales people in one capacity or another. The relationship is what is essential to any

STOP MANAGING YOUR SALES PROCESS LIKE YOUR SEX LIFE

sales cycle. What kind of relationship do you have with your prospects?

STOP MANAGING YOUR SALES PROCESS LIKE YOUR SEX LIFE

STOP MANAGING YOUR SALES PROCESS LIKE YOUR SEX LIFE

Dating/Sales Tip 1: The Infamous One Night Stand

Seriously?! Are you really spending precious time and money at networking events to meet and connect with extraordinary prospects, pass out your expensive business cards (IF you're really investing in your brand- that's another book), introduce yourself, gather a stack of business cards (IF you're working the room-that's another book), committing to reaching out to each person that could/should use your services or product and NOT ever ever ever follow-up?

What an absolutely waste of time! Theirs and yours. If you're not serious about committing to forming a relationship with the people at the organizations that can drive revenue to you and your business, why

STOP MANAGING YOUR SALES PROCESS LIKE YOUR SEX LIFE

bother? Go to the bar to drink and pick up chicks or guys. Get out the business networking pool and leave it to the ones like me who are really interested in taking our business to the next level. You know-those of us who are ever so serious about working to add clients and logos to our list of accounts in our portfolios.

Business 101- Remember why you are at the event.

If you're not "feeling it", if you don't want to be bothered with people, then don't go. Use your time to work on other marketing options and follow-up items, such as:

-Make cold-calls or send follow-up emails

-Create your next day's to-do list

-Update your pipeline

STOP MANAGING YOUR SALES PROCESS LIKE YOUR SEX LIFE

-Familiarize yourself with the competition

-Think of alternate branding solutions for your business

Sometimes we truly don't "feel it" and that's ok. Just don't make it a habit. If you never "feel it" you could end up homeless and hungry. Time and money are important to any business, ESPECIALLY if you're an entrepreneur and working with a start-up. Use your resources wisely and please leave the one night-stands out of your business routines. Follow-up with your contacts. Schedule appointments. Do what you've committed to doing for/with them.

STOP MANAGING YOUR SALES PROCESS LIKE YOUR SEX LIFE

STOP MANAGING YOUR SALES PROCESS LIKE YOUR SEX LIFE

Dating/Sales Tip 2: You're a Stalker-Never a Closer

Stop lurking! You know all that you need to know about that prospect. You have linked up with them on LinkedIn. You have formed a great relationship with your contact's "gatekeeper". You have the Decision Makers business card with their direct phone and email contact information. You have the service or product they need. You pretty much follow them faithfully on Facebook without actually sending a "friend" request. (Don't do that by the way-that's creepy). What the heck are you waiting for?

MOVE IN. Set-up the face-to-face meeting.

STOP MANAGING YOUR SALES PROCESS LIKE YOUR SEX LIFE

LISTEN. During the meeting, after an intro of why you're qualified to sit in this setting with them. SHUT UP and listen to their needs.

PARTNER. Tell your contact how doing business with you will improve their current situation. Be creative

LISTEN. You have two ears-doing this twice won't hurt. Any challenges/resistance? If yes, ensure you fully understand what you need to solve for.

AFFIRM. Close the deal by confirming you're both on the same page and CONFIRM next steps (action items, follow-up meetings, etc...)

STOP MANAGING YOUR SALES PROCESS LIKE YOUR SEX LIFE

Your *Stalker* days are over-move in to transition to *Closer*.

You're ready!

STOP MANAGING YOUR SALES PROCESS LIKE YOUR SEX LIFE

STOP MANAGING YOUR SALES PROCESS LIKE YOUR SEX LIFE

Dating/Sales Tip 3: Are you going to date him/her to death?

Commitment issues? You've taken them to breakfast meetings, lunch meetings and treated them to dinners. You've sent them 'Get well' flowers, 'Happy Birthday' emails, and doughnuts and other goodies to their office staff.

Believe me, they get it! They know you *like* them and want their business. They notice the effort. Since you're all on the same page now-let's just bop the elephant in the room in the eye. Ask for the deal. Ask for the contract. Go in for the close. This business is all about closing not dating your prospects to death. They have a social life for that.

STOP MANAGING YOUR SALES PROCESS LIKE YOUR SEX LIFE

Don't become annoying AND don't stop all of the schmoozing once you get their business. We'll talk about that later in the book.

STOP MANAGING YOUR SALES PROCESS LIKE YOUR SEX LIFE

STOP MANAGING YOUR SALES PROCESS LIKE YOUR SEX LIFE

STOP MANAGING YOUR SALES PROCESS LIKE YOUR SEX LIFE

Dating/Sales Tip 4: The Booty Call

Your prospect calls you when they need you but won't commit. So you're convenient. You make it so easy. They use you when they are in a bind, a crunch…when they are "horny". You've proven yourself over and over, again when this happens and have yet to get a commitment from your contact? Why?

You have to know your worth. While I admit this is a fine line when working with a prospect and you should tread lightly, but if your track record to perform with last minute, "rush" requests is always top-notch, I'd say you deserve some level of commitment and consistent business with this person and their organization. Perhaps suggest that they run a dual/parallel program with the competition and your

STOP MANAGING YOUR SALES PROCESS LIKE YOUR SEX LIFE

organization to allow them to compare your overall performance.

Again, be creative. Don't be afraid to remind your contact of how you've partnered without an actual contract when they needed you most and ask them to be the same type of partner to you. What do you have to lose? What's worse than being a booty call?

STOP MANAGING YOUR SALES PROCESS LIKE YOUR SEX LIFE

STOP MANAGING YOUR SALES PROCESS LIKE YOUR SEX LIFE

STOP MANAGING YOUR SALES PROCESS LIKE YOUR SEX LIFE

Dating/Sales Tip 5: Rejection-They Don't Want You

This hurts. Rejectionland is never a fun place to be, but let's be real, being rejected is part of the sales process. You'll kiss a lot of frogs before you finally find your princess or prince=client. WHEN they politely say no or no, thank you despite your fearless efforts to overcome their objections, it's time to recognize that it's not time for this relationship to move forward. It doesn't necessarily mean you'll never end up in "happy ever after land". It does mean NOT now. Respect the client's decision and don't pester them. Give them some space. Put a reminder in your calendar to follow-up in about a year, especially if they are under contract and are "happy" in their current relationship with another vendor. If you can get intel of when the contract expires, it may be a good idea to revive your reach out to the client a few months prior to this timeframe.

STOP MANAGING YOUR SALES PROCESS LIKE YOUR SEX LIFE

Again, don't be a pest and don't be annoying. They'll remember it and will be totally turned off. There's a need for finesse to manage this part of the process. Use your best judgment. If it would bother you to be contacted in the same manner in which you are "attacking" I meant pursuing your client-then it's perhaps time to pull up and fall back.

Move on to the next one in your pipeline. You have something someone wants and needs. Focus on those in your queue.

STOP MANAGING YOUR SALES PROCESS LIKE YOUR SEX LIFE

STOP MANAGING YOUR SALES PROCESS LIKE YOUR SEX LIFE

STOP MANAGING YOUR SALES PROCESS LIKE YOUR SEX LIFE

Dating/Sales Tip 6: The Proposal

So you finally asked for the deal. They've "said" yes. Hmmmm...I've learned in my experience of the sales game that a verbal agreement is only as good as the ink it's written with. It means absolutely NOTHING. Get a contract in front of your contact immediately. Understand that negotiations are part of most contract processes. While you have the Decision Maker engaged, make sure you keep the contracting part of the process moving expeditiously.

Remind the client how excited you are about the deal and partnering with them. They like the right level of attention and a professional reminder that they've made the right decision to announce their plans to be in a "relationship" with you and your organization.

STOP MANAGING YOUR SALES PROCESS LIKE YOUR SEX LIFE

The last thing you want to do is to give them time to mull over their decision and have a change of heart. You're engaged. Finalize the event by getting a signed contract.

Congratulations!

STOP MANAGING YOUR SALES PROCESS LIKE YOUR SEX LIFE

STOP MANAGING YOUR SALES PROCESS LIKE YOUR SEX LIFE

Dating/Sales Tip 7: The Anniversary-contract extension/renewal

You have a contract. Thing are going well. Probably pretty status quo like many marriages after a while. Keep the fire in the relationship. Continue to date your client even after you're "married" and the contract has been signed. A divorce could be detrimental to your reputation and your revenue stream. Don't take your client's business for granted. Like any significant other, your client wants to continue to feel special. They need to feel the "love".

Ensure you're reaching out on those special days (birthdays, company anniversaries, etc…) Continue to wine and dine the client. Send doughnuts and/or goodies "just because". I've found that even when there have been hiccups with service deliveries, the relationship you've established with the client is priceless. Maintaining this level of the relationship may get you an invitation to a RFP (Request For Proposal) bid that you don't deserve.

Gentle reminder- Make sure you keep a calendar reminder of the expiration date of your current contract. At least 6 months before expiration, you want to make sure you're actively courting your client.

STOP MANAGING YOUR SALES PROCESS LIKE YOUR SEX LIFE

STOP MANAGING YOUR SALES PROCESS LIKE YOUR SEX LIFE

STOP MANAGING YOUR SALES PROCESS LIKE YOUR SEX LIFE

So that's about it. I knowwwwwww-it's not rocket science but it really is that simple. Keep your sex-life in the bedroom and run your business like it's a business. Stalking is sooo not attractive and being a "booty call" can't be fulfilling long term. You're better than that and don't be afraid to tactfully tell your client this. Sometimes it's okay to walk away if your value isn't recognized by a particular person or organization. It may not be the relationship for you. You can't sleep with everyone you meet. Unless you're running a brothel.

STOP MANAGING YOUR SALES PROCESS LIKE YOUR SEX LIFE

Thank you for taking the time for reading my book and for your purchase.

Please visit my website: www.Luncefordlistens.com to see how I can help you build your brand, revive your brand, become your accountability partner or create a custom solution for your unique need.

"FIRST, we listen, THEN we execute!"

Sincerely,

Erika L. Lunceford

STOP MANAGING YOUR SALES PROCESS LIKE YOUR SEX LIFE

www.ingramcontent.com/pod-product-compliance
Lightning Source LLC
Chambersburg PA
CBHW070724180526
45167CB00004B/1611